CLASSICAL
mood

Bittersweet
Memories

Bittersweet Memories

This volume of *In Classical Mood* captures both the sheer tenderness and the utter heartbreak of the bittersweet memories that seem to follow us through life. Brought together here are twelve pieces of music designed to reveal the many different facets of those unforgettable moments—from Samuel Barber's melancholy *Adagio for Strings* and Mozart's sublime *Piano Concerto No.21*, to Sibelius's haunting *Swan of Tuonela* and Chopin's tender *Étude No.3 in E Major*. But be warned: Even the driest of eyes may not stay dry for too long!

THE LISTENER'S GUIDE – WHAT THE SYMBOLS MEAN

THE COMPOSERS
Their lives... their loves.. their legacies...

THE MUSIC
Explanation... analysis... interpretation...

THE INSPIRATION
How works of genius came to be written

THE BACKGROUND
People, places, and events linked to the music

© MCMXCVI IMP AB   In Classical Mood™   IMP AB, produced under license by IMP Inc.   Printed in China.   US P 2201 12 009

Contents

SAMUEL BARBER
1910–1981

Adagio for Strings

From the first melancholy chords, *Adagio for Strings* powerfully conveys the feeling of emptiness that can accompany a bittersweet memory. The haunting melody and shifting harmonies roll on through the piece like a dark and desolate landscape. As the music reaches its climax, there is a sudden dramatic pause, which says more about the despair of loneliness than words could ever do, before the dramatic opening theme returns.

CAUGHT ON FILM

American composer Samuel Barber wrote his *Adagio* in the late 1930s during the Great Depression. Half a century later, the sorrowful and intense message of the music found new expression in two of the most moving films of the 1980s—David Lynch's *The Elephant Man* (1980) and Oliver Stone's portrayal of the horrific experiences of U.S. troops in the Vietnam War in *Platoon* (1986).

MILITARY SERVICE

In April 1943, during World War II, Barber *(below)* was drafted for military service and assigned to the Army Air Force *(right)*. His first year was spent at Fort Worth, Texas, where he continued to compose. The outcome was two works specially commissioned by the Air Force—the *Commando March*, written for the symphonic wind band, and the *Second Symphony*, which he dedicated to the USAAF. Barber was never satisfied with this symphony, which he attempted to revise, only to withdraw it twenty-four years later. The second movement has survived, however, with the title "Night Flight."

ROMANTIC STYLE

Barber's lyrical music had more in common with the Romantic era than the modernist mid-20th century, which may account for its lasting appeal. After the war, he wrote two of the few American operas ever to be staged at New York City's Metropolitan Opera House: *Vanessa*, which won the Pulitzer Prize in 1958, and *Antony and Cleopatra*, which opened the new Metropolitan Opera House *(left)* at Lincoln Center in 1966.

KEY NOTES

Adagio for Strings *was originally created for a string quartet, but at the suggestion of friend and Italian maestro Arturo Toscanini, Barber later reworked the slow movement to be played by an orchestra.*

WOLFGANG AMADEUS MOZART
1756–1791

Piano Concerto No. 21 in C Major

K467: SECOND MOVEMENT

This tender and reflective slow movement is from Mozart's most famous piano concerto, which is now commonly referred to as *Elvira Madigan* because of its use in the film of the same name. The charm and elegance of the opening melody rises and falls against a plucked string accompaniment, before giving way to delicate and more thoughtful piano passages that bring about daydreams of "what might have been."

MOZART'S PIANO CONCERTOS

Mozart produced no fewer than twenty-seven concertos for solo piano and orchestra, twelve of which were composed between 1784 and 1786. Some of Mozart's concertos were written for his friends and pupils, and others for himself. He often left gaps in the piano part so that he could improvise sections (*cadenzas*) during a performance. The melancholic nature of this movement may reflect the difficult time that Mozart experienced in 1784, when he was stricken by a serious illness and became plagued by thoughts of death. Not surprisingly, this was a time, too, when he became much more interested in religion.

Mozart was a master of the keyboard, both as a pianist and as a composer.

ELVIRA MADIGAN

The nickname *Elvira Madigan* originates from a romantic Swedish film from 1967 that has a tragic ending. The film was much praised for

Left: *A scene from Elvira Madigan, starring Pia Degermark and Thommy Berggren.*

the beauty of its photography and its lovely natural settings, which Mozart's music did much to enhance.

SIR EDWARD ELGAR *1857–1934*

Cello Concerto in E Minor

OPUS 85: THIRD MOVEMENT

Few instruments can express bittersweet memories as poignantly as the cello. And in this slow movement of the concerto, which was written to mourn the passing of an era, Elgar uses the cello's expressive power to wonderful effect. The piece is all the more powerful for its simplicity: Subdued strings and the absence of heavy brass add to the meditative quality, leaving the cello to sing its rich yet questioning melody alone.

TRANSATLANTIC

The Englishman Elgar made several trips across the Atlantic. The most notable one was with his wife, Alice, in June 1905, when as an internationally renowned musician he received an honorary degree from Yale University.

MOUNTING SADNESS

Like many artists, Elgar was deeply affected by World War I. Not only did the war's death toll greatly sadden him, but it also marked the end of the Edwardian era with which he had so closely identified. In 1919, too, Elgar's beloved wife, Alice *(right, inset)*, became ill, dying a year later. Many critics believe that the somber strains of this concerto reflect his mounting sense of isolation in a world that had changed forever.

THE CELLO

From the eloquence of its lower register to the heart-rending tone of its higher notes, the cello has a unique capacity to tug at the heartstrings of human emotion. Surprisingly, few cello concertos were written during the Romantic era. But those that were—by Brahms, Schumann, Tchaikovsky, and Dvořák—do great credit to the richness of the instrument. Although written in the 20th century, Elgar's masterpiece crowns the tradition of Romantic cello concertos and forms a moving farewell to a vanished age.

KEY NOTES

The premiere of the Cello Concerto *in* October 1919 at the Queen's Hall, London, was the last of Elgar's premieres attended by Alice. She died on April 7, 1920, after which he wrote very little.

JEAN SIBELIUS *1865–1957*

The Swan of Tuonela

No.3, Opus 22

Inspired by a Finnish legend, this wonderfully impressionistic piece of music depicts a mythical swan that swims the dark river surrounding Tuonela—the Finnish equivalent of the Greek Underworld. To win his intended bride, the hero of the story must kill the swan. But in the end it is the hero who dies, and the swan brings his body away to its final resting place. Here the swan's mournful song is conveyed by the hauntingly beautiful tones of the cor anglais, while the undulating texture of the strings perfectly captures the empty stillness of this bittersweet tale.

A SYMPHONIC POEM

Sibelius originally composed "The Swan of Tuonela" in 1893 as the prelude to an opera, which he left unfinished. Later the piece was published as one of four symphonic poems—short pieces, similar to single-movement symphonies—which were entitled *Legends for Orchestra*. Sibelius based all of these pieces on stories from the Finnish national epic poem "Kalevala."

FINLAND AWAKES

In 1899, six years after he wrote the *The Swan of Tuonela*, the thirty-four-year-old Sibelius *(below)* became caught up in the intense political unrest that was sweeping Finland. The country had fallen under Tsarist Russian control in February of that year and free speech was prohibited. At a celebration in Helsinki, in aid of a press pension fund, Sibelius conducted the first performance of a new work entitled *Finland Awakes*. The song created such patriotic feelings that Russia banned the piece. He revised it the following year, renaming it *Finlandia*, and as the Finnish fought for and won their independence, it was heralded as the national anthem.

Above: *Helsinki, the Finnish capital and a hotbed of nationalism around the turn of the 20th century.*

INSPIRED BY FINNISH LEGENDS

From his early days as a student, Sibelius had a deep love for the mythology and folklore of his native country. He took an almost

A Finnish tapestry (left) *depicting a scene from the poem "Kalevala."*

obsessive interest in the folk legends of the "Kalevala," which provided inspiration throughout his career right up to his last great composition, *Tapiola*, in 1926.

9

THE SILENT DECADES

Thanks to *Finlandia*, Sibelius became a national hero. As a result, he was showered with praise. In 1926, the Finnish government donated a large sum from a nationwide fund as a show of appreciation and awarded him a state pension for life. On his 90th birthday the composer received over 1,200 telegrams, along with gifts from Scandinavian monarchs and cigars from Sir Winston Churchill. Despite the adulation, Sibelius's life was marked by depression and heavy drinking. Fame could not dispel the sadness that caused him to spend the last thirty years of his life in relative solitude. Remarkably, from 1930 to his death in 1957, he did not write one note of music.

Sibelius lived for many years in his villa, Ainola (above), in Järvenpää near Helsinki. He was known for his fine collection of cigars (right).

PAYING HIS WAY

Sibelius made his one and only trip to the U.S. in 1914, and the visit proved to be one of the highlights of his career. Never before had he been treated as such a celebrity, with no expense spared. Ironically, Sibelius was in dire financial straits at home, and this prompted him to plan another visit to America to help pay off his debts. But the advent of World War I put an end to his hopes of an immediate return trip.

KEY NOTES

Sibelius's Fourth Symphony *caused an uproar in the U.S. when it was premiered by Toscanini in 1911. After the audience greeted it with derision, Toscanini defiantly announced that he would immediately play the piece again!*

EDVARD GRIEG *1843–1907*

Peer Gynt

SOLVEIG'S SONG

Derived from a Norwegian folk song, this much-loved piece from Grieg's incidental music for *Peer Gynt* tenderly expresses the sweet sadness of longing. The hushed strings add a sense of delicacy to the scene while yearning phrases on the violins supply the tune. In the midst of Solveig's sorrow comes a quicker, brighter melody, reminding her of the joys of love. But this soon dies away, and the original melancholy tune returns.

WAITING IN VAIN

In the story of *Peer Gynt*, Solveig sacrifices everything in the name of love and journeys across the snow to Peer's remote hut in the forest to be with him. But he is away on his travels. This song expresses Solveig's longing as she waits patiently for his return.

FRÉDÉRIC CHOPIN *1810–1849*

Étude No.3 in E Major

OPUS 10

This piece is one of the most moving, perhaps the saddest, of all Chopin's études (studies). It begins with a musical interpretation of tenderly spoken words of love and affection, beautifully conveyed by the conversational melody, with its short, balanced phrases. In the middle section, the music quickly rises to a turbulent pitch, with notes cascading over one another in a passionate display of anger and frustration. Then the outburst subsides, leaving the tender opening melody to end the piece.

CHOPIN THE PATRIOT

Chopin *(right, inset)* grew up in the Polish capital of Warsaw *(right)*, where he came to cherish the customs and culture of his country from an early age. He was a staunch patriot, and much of his work—particularly his *mazurkas* (Polish peasant dances)—was inspired by Polish folk music. In 1831, while Chopin was living in Paris, Warsaw fell to the Russians. This threw him into a mood of despondency that no amount of Parisian high living could alleviate. The turmoil that Chopin felt is reflected in much of the music he composed at this time, notably the "Revolutionary" étude, the twelfth and last in the Opus 10 series.

Above: *Entry of the Russian troops into Warsaw after the failed revolution of 1830.*

EVERLASTING MEMORY

The young Chopin fell passionately in love with Constantia Gladkowska *(left)*, a pupil at the Warsaw Conservatory whom he worshiped from a distance. In his letters, he speaks of her as a major inspiration in his music, particularly in his First Piano Concerto. Constantia eventually married someone else. It is likely that this étude recalls Chopin's bittersweet memory of his love for her—a love that he would carry to his grave.

KEY NOTES

The étude, *from the French for* "exercise" *or* "study," *was a popular form of piano composition in the early 19th century. Chopin's études were more than just exercises and took the form out of the school room onto the concert platform.*

ANTONIN DVOŘÁK *1841–1904*

String Quartet in F Major

OPUS 96, "AMERICAN": SECOND MOVEMENT

The mournful slow movement of this string quartet reflects Dvořák's deep nostalgia for his homeland, Czechoslovakia *(right)*. There is a Bohemian flavor to the opening, with a subdued, off-beat rhythm supporting the violin's gypsy-like melody. The cello then picks up the theme, and as the tension builds, the two instruments enter into a passionate dialogue. The cello takes the last solo, recalling the nostalgic feel of the opening as the notes descend from the top register into darker depths.

NOT IMPRESSED

Dvořák's father, a butcher by trade, was not happy about his son becoming a musician. At fifteen, the young Antonin sought to change his father's mind by writing a polka for the town band. But lack of rehearsal meant that the performance was a dreadful din. His father was even less impressed!

Longing for Home

Dvořák composed this string quartet during the summer of 1893 while on vacation in the Czech immigrant community of Spillville, Iowa. The town was a welcome retreat from the noise and busy schedules of New York, where he had just completed "From the New World," and he was joined on vacation by his sister, wife, and six children. Dvořák found the experience not only inspiring but also uplifting. Long walks among the fields and orchards of Spillville with his fellow countrymen did much to curb the longing for his native Bohemia *(top right)* that plagued him during his three-year stay in America.

The Kneisel Quartet (right) *premiered the* String Quartet in F Major *in Boston, Mass. on January 1, 1894.*

American Influence

The *String Quartet in F Major* was given the title *American Quartet* because it was thought to be influenced by American music. The title might equally well apply to its sister piece, the *String Quintet in E-flat*, which was also written during Dvořák's stay in Spillville, Iowa. Emotionally, though, both pieces are a much stronger reflection of the Bohemian composer's fond memories of his far-off native land.

Key Notes

Dvořák scored the American Quartet from start to finish in three days and finished writing it in fifteen. He wrote on the score, "Thank God! I am content: It has gone very quickly."

MAURICE RAVEL *1875–1937*

Pavane pour une infante défunte

Written for the piano in 1899, and orchestrated ten years later, this reflective yet balanced piece, tinged with sadness, is the perfect showcase for the exceptional talents of the French composer Maurice Ravel. Instead of relying on a single instrument to carry the melody, Ravel employs a rich variety of instrumental color— horns, woodwind, and strings—in every phrase, giving the work a uniquely liquid form and feel.

ROYAL CUSTOMS

"Pavan for a dead Infanta" (Infanta being a Spanish princess) was inspired by a Spanish court custom involving a solemn ceremonial dance during a time of royal mourning. Ravel did not actually have any particular princess in mind.

MAN OF FASHION

Born in the Basque country of southwest France, Maurice Ravel studied at the Paris Conservatoire de Musique. Very much the "man about town," he became the darling of Parisian café society

(right). He joined a group of like-minded young artists in Paris, whose regular meetings gave them the chance to discuss ideas and collaborate on projects. He prided himself on having the best collection of neckties in Paris and was greatly disappointed when he visited the U.S. and discovered that his ties were unfashionably long—he had to snip the ends off!

PUBLIC ANNOUNCEMENT

In 1921, the French government finally decided to recognize Ravel's achievements by awarding him the much-prized *Légion d'Honneur*. Unfortunately, the award was announced publicly before Ravel himself had been informed of the decision and he promptly declined to accept it. One honor he did accept, however, was an honorary doctorate from Oxford University in 1931 *(right)*.

THE SWISS WATCHMAKER

Stravinsky once described Ravel *(left)* as "the Swiss watchmaker" of music, because of Ravel's painstaking attention to detail. Ravel himself described a work of art as "a ripened conception where no detail has been left to chance." And so it was that he developed his own method of composing, which was central to his style. He perfected small, self-contained "blocks" of music, then assembled them into larger, more complex structures—much like the many moving parts of a watch! Thus it was that he earned Stravinsky's approval.

TOUR OF AMERICA

Although Ravel traveled abroad in his youth, it was not until he was in his his fifties that he ventured across the Atlantic. His four-month tour of the U.S. in 1928 was an enormous success: His numerous concerts and piano recitals received an enthusiastic reception, and he was introduced to celebrities from the worlds of art and showbiz (including George Gershwin, whose work he much admired). Ravel's trip across America must have been hard work, but in fact he found that it had one unexpected benefit: A long-time insomniac, he confessed that traveling on the long-distance overnight trains gave him the best night's sleep that he'd had since childhood!

KEY NOTES

On hearing French pianist Charles Oulmont play Pavane pour une infante défunte *at a painfully slow pace*, Ravel tersely stated that it was the Infanta who was dead and not the pavane!

Johann Sebastian Bach
1685–1750

Sonata in G Minor

(For Viola da Gamba)
BWV 1029: Second Movement

This melancholy, yet dignified slow movement takes the form of a dialogue between the viola da gamba and the harpsichord. Like two former lovers in search of reconciliation, there is a certain nobility in the viola da gamba's melody that finds a sensitive response in the harpsichord's delicate, lingering phrases.

The Viola da Gamba

The viola da gamba, or "bass viol," is played between the knees like a cello, but has a shape closer to that of a large violin *(above right)*. The viola da gamba was superseded by the broader-toned, more versatile cello during the 19th century.

Key Notes

For many years this Sonata remained obscure. But in 1990 the piece became well known in the movie world after being featured in the successful British film Truly Madly Deeply.

HENRY PURCELL *1659–1695*

Dido and Aeneas

DIDO'S LAMENT

With nothing but death to look forward to, the anguish of desertion is transformed into noble passion in this most evocative of songs from an opera by the 17th-century English composer Henry Purcell. Against the simple background of a delicate, four-part orchestral accompaniment, Dido's impassioned welcoming of death floats majestically through the still air. "Remember me," she sings on just a single note, "but ah! forget my fate."

A TRAGIC LAMENT

Set in Carthage, an ancient city in North Africa, Purcell's opera is based on an episode from Roman poet Virgil's *Aeneid*. Deserted by her lover Aeneas, who has sailed to Italy in search of his destiny, and with only her faithful sister, Belinda, for company, Dido sings this tragic and passionate lament. Shortly afterward she dies, heartbroken.

REVOLUTIONARY OPERA

Dido and Aeneas (1689) is the first true English opera (and the last until Britten's *Peter Grimes* in 1945). England had a long tradition of spectacular staged events, known as *masques*, with music, songs, and dramatic scenes, but hardly any real links between the various elements. The strong connection between the music and the drama in *Dido and Aeneas* is unique for English music of this period. Purcell did not compose any more operas, although he did write five semi-operas, in which the music acts as an accompaniment to the play. He also wrote incidental music for popular dramas of the time by writers such as Dryden and Congreve. His early death probably robbed the stage of other great operas.

Purcell (below) died in London at the age of thirty-six and was buried in Westminster Abbey (right).

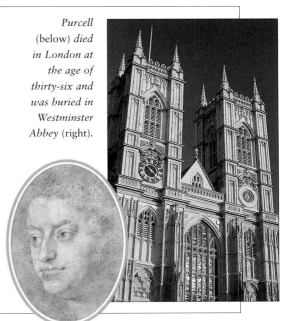

JOSIAS PRIEST

Dido and Aeneas was originally commissioned to be performed by "young gentlewomen" at a boarding school in Chelsea, London. The school was run by Josias Priest, a dancing master who is thought to have arranged all the opera's dances himself. In the following years, Purcell and Priest continued their successful partnership and brought dance arrangements of some of Purcell's other dramatic music to the London stage.

> **KEY NOTES**
>
> The tension in "Dido's Lament" is partly achieved by using a ground bass—a line that repeats itself, creating tension with the changing harmonies above it. A ground bass also adds continuity to the song as a whole.

FRANZ LISZT *1811–1886*

Consolation No.3 in D-flat Major

(FOR PIANO)

*L*iszt wrote all six of his *Consolations*, of which this is the best known, between 1849 and 1850 while living in Weimar, Germany, with Princess Carolyne Sayn-Wittgenstein. It is easy to imagine that the gentle and dreamy flow of the music—one of the most tender pieces ever written for solo piano—is inspired by the composer's affection for the princess, but it is bittersweet because she was in fact married to another. There is also a deeper level of inspiration at work. The piece breathes an introspection that signifies the profoundly religious side of Liszt's personality.

PRINCESS CAROLYNE

Princess Carolyne Sayn-Wittgenstein *(below)* first met Liszt in Kiev, in the Ukraine, in 1847 on what was to be his last concert tour. His playing had a profound effect on the twenty-eight-year-old princess, but she was to have an even greater effect on him! Unfortunately for Liszt, Carolyne was still married at the time to a Russian prince and had a child, which meant that Carolyne and Liszt were not free to marry. The Princess actually managed to get permission from the Pope to divorce, but at the last stage it was mysteriously revoked. On hearing of Liszt's death, Princess Carolyne immediately withdrew into a life of solitude. She died seven months later.

Above: *Liszt's grave in Bayreuth, Bavaria.*
Left: *Princess Carolyne, who loved him to the end.*

THE WEIMAR DAYS

Weimar was a thriving center for Germany's thinkers and artists during the time that Liszt and Princess Carolyne lived there, from 1848 to 1861. It was a stimulating and highly productive period for Liszt, who kept open house for distinguished musicians, writers, and philosophers from all over Europe. Among the constant stream of visitors was the English novelist George Eliot, who wrote of Liszt that "Genius, benevolence, and tenderness beam from his whole countenance."

KEY NOTES

Franz Liszt took the name "Consolation" from the title of a poem. All six of Liszt's Consolations, which were completed in 1850, are reflective in nature. They are similar to nocturnes in both style and mood.

MAX BRUCH *1838–1920*

Violin Concerto No.1 in G Minor

OPUS 26: SECOND MOVEMENT

Through the orchestra's muted strings, the solo violin rises, like a bird, to a fervent climax. The violin then reappears briefly with a lighter tune before the original theme returns, revealing why this slow movement is considered one of the most moving pieces that has ever been written for violin and orchestra.

24

UNFULFILLED DESTINY

 After he wrote an overture and some chamber music at eleven, a symphony that won the Frankfurt Mozart Foundation Prize at fourteen, and an opera when he was twenty, it was clear that German-born Max Bruch *(below)* was destined to achieve greatness as a composer. His professional career looked promising, too: He was appointed Director of Music in Koblenz, after which he became chief conductor at the Sonderhausen court. Recognition of Bruch as a composer came when he was given a master class in composition at the Berlin Academy from 1891 until his retirement in 1910. In spite of his popularity with his contemporaries, his music failed to win long-lasting success. Today his fame rests almost entirely on this violin concerto.

MAESTRO'S APPROVAL

 Bruch had some misgivings about his *Violin Concerto in G Minor* and, following its premiere on April 24, 1866, he made a number of revisions to the score. Concerned that the newly revised work was too unconventional, he sent the manuscript to Joseph Joachim *(below)*, who was one of the leading violinists of the time and himself an acclaimed composer. Impressed, Joachim reassured Bruch that his work "fully justified" being called a concerto and insisted on performing it in Bremen in 1868.

KEY NOTES

 Bruch later wrote two more violin concertos and a delightful Scottish Fantasy. *Though they all have their admirers, none has enjoyed the huge popularity of* Violin Concerto No.1.

Credits & Acknowledgments

PICTURE CREDITS

Cover /Title and Contents Pages/ IBC: Images Colour Library

AKG London: 5(r), 14, 21(tc), 25(l); The Art Museum of the Ateneum, Helsinki: 9(bl); Bridgeman Art Library, London/Prado, Madrid: 16; Roy Miles Gallery, London: 22; Corbis-Bettmann: 3(tl); UPI: 3(bl); The Elgar Foundation: 7(cr); ET Archive: 13(tr); Eye Ubiquitous: 2; Mary Evans Picture Library: 17(tr); Chris Fairclough Colour Library/Ian Macfadyen: 8; Fine Art Photographic Library: 4; Ronald Grant Archive: 5(l); Robert Harding Picture Library/ Mark Mawson: 6; Richard Ashworth: 15(tr); Hulton Getty: 3(tr); Images Colour Library: 12, 21(tr); Lebrecht Collection: 9(cl), 10(tr & cr), 13(bl), 15(cr), 17(l & br), 23(tc & tr), 25(r); MC Picture Library: 7(bl); Courtesy of The National Museum, Helsinki: 9(tr); NHPA/Stephen Dalton: 24; Royal College of Music: 13(c), 18(t); Sibeliusmuseum, Abo: 9(tl); Sotheby's: 11, 19, 20, 22; World Pictures: 7(tr).

All illustrations and symbols: John See